CONTENTS

1 INTRODUCTION

The term *monopoly* is generally taken to mean a situation where a single supplier, or group of suppliers acting together, controls a substantial part of the total supply of a commodity and, by virtue of this control, is able to manipulate price, quality, or other conditions of sale of that commodity.

The term *restrictive trade practices* is taken to mean the variety of marketing practices used by monopolists to establish, strengthen, or exploit their control over the market. Monopoly refers to a particular type of market situation while restrictive practices are the means by which this situation is created and maintained.

Many students are misled by the derivation of the word monopoly into thinking solely in terms of a unified monopoly. Monopoly is a market situation where we have a single *supplier* and not necessarily a single producer. There may be a number of independent producers, but, if they combine in order to market their products, we have a single supplier. The situation is changing, however, and increasing attention is now being paid to the large dominant firm.

The basic textbook *Understanding Economics* deals with the theoretical aspects of monopoly and other types of market situation; in this book we are concerned mainly with public policy and monopoly power. In presenting the arguments in favour of monopoly, as well as those against, it is hoped to provide a better understanding of why Britain was rather late in taking action to control monopoly, why the controls have taken their present form, and why some of the measures appear to be rather contradictory. It is also the aim of this text to provide an appreciation of the current problems of a society in which the government is trying to obtain the great economic advantages of large scale production whilst, at the same time, avoiding the disadvantages of monopoly.

The legislation is presented in some detail but the main emphasis throughout is on the aims of the legislation, the problems faced by those who have to take decisions, and the results achieved.

The exercises at the end of this book are intended to provide the student with scope for investigation, analysis, and presentation of work in this important and very interesting subject.

2 THE STRUCTURE OF MONOPOLY

1 Monopoly power

According to the original meaning of the word, monopoly exists when there is only one seller of a particular commodity. Actually, it is not difficult for a producer to put himself in this position. With the common practices of branding and the use of trade marks it is relatively easy to become a sole supplier. For example, only one firm has the legal right to produce Cadbury's chocolate, and only ICI can supply Dulux paint.

If, however, the branded commodity has several close substitutes, the producer has very little power to squeeze the buyers. They have the freedom to switch to the substitute products. The power to raise prices and earn abnormal profits is determined by the ability of the monopolist to make buyers dependent upon his supplies. He must be able, in some way, to restrict the availability of close substitutes. A supplier is able to exercise monopoly power, therefore, only if he can eliminate, or seriously restrict, competition. The extent of monopoly power depends upon the degree to which the monopolist is affected by the actions of sellers of similar products to his own, and upon the degree to which the demand for his product may be affected by new sellers.

It is difficult to measure the extent of monopoly power. In practice two alternative methods tend to be used. One is a concentration ratio which shows the proportion of the total market controlled by the three or four largest firms in the industry. This idea uses the share of the market as an indication of market power. Another method takes account of the level of profits. If profits are high, and remain high, it is regarded as indirect evidence that a monopoly situation exists. Monopoly power is seen as the ability to earn long-run abnormal profits.

It should be borne in mind that the existence of a single firm,[1] or a high concentration ratio, or even high profits, do not prove the existence of monopoly power: they indicate no more than a possibility that it may exist.

2 Establishing a monopoly position
a Economies of scale and competition

The essence of monopoly, as we have seen, is the power to restrict the emergence of potential competitors. There are several methods by which this objective may be achieved.

In many ways the recent industrial and commercial revolutions have made possible the growth of monopolies. The development

---

[1] In the case of a single firm in the domestic market, monopoly power may be severely limited by unrestricted imports.

of the limited liability company, the growth of an effective capital market, and the increased efficiency of stock exchanges, have made it possible to finance very large industrial enterprises. Technological progress in manufacturing, transport, and communications has provided the scope for very significant economies of scale. When such developments take place in a private enterprise economy where price competition is effective, one would expect − on the basis of the survival of the fittest − the emergence of the very large corporation. The efficient and enterprising firms would make the maximum use of the advantages of larger scale production and eliminate their less efficient rivals by price competition. Competition would lead, paradoxically, to monopoly. This is, in fact, what was happening in the United States in the last quarter of the nineteenth century, where it led to the famous Sherman Anti-Trust Act of 1890.

In many industries the barriers to entry are technical barriers. Technical advances in such industries as chemicals, oil, motor manufacturing, tyres, and many others, have placed a formidable premium on size. Technical economies of scale in these industries are most impressive and have led to the emergence of a few giant firms which have, between them, the greater part of the total market. The optimum size of the firm is very large and a few firms of this size can, quite effectively, meet the total demand. Any new firm wanting to enter such an industry would, in order to compete effectively with existing firms, have to commence operations on a scale as large as theirs. But this would lead to a large increase in total output and to cut-throat competition between giants. The size of the capital sum required to set up such a firm, and the probable consequences of such action, are effective deterrents to entry.

We have seen how technical and commercial progress, together with the forces of competition, can lead to the emergence of dominant firms. Where one firm rises to dominate an industry it will have monopoly powers − the ability to influence total output and hence market price. Where a few large firms succeed in capturing the greater part of the market we have a situation which might or might not result in monopoly power. If the firms choose to compete (a situation of oligopoly) then competition might be very fierce indeed. It is possible, however, that the very prospect of such competition will lead firms into collusion and the formation of some kind of monopoly organisation.

b Legal powers to restrict entry
Probably the most complete security against competition is provided by a legal prohibition of new entrants to an industry.

This form of monopoly has a long history. The charters granted by the Crown to the great overseas trading companies (e.g. The East India Company and The Hudson's Bay Company) conferred monopoly trading privileges.

Further examples of monopoly positions protected by the law are those which rest upon patent rights. In more recent times we have seen the granting of legally exclusive rights to supply to the nationalised industries. It must be made clear that where entry into an industry is legally prohibited it does not mean the absence of competition. Holders of patents often find that others may design some similar product which, although it does not infringe the original patent, effectively destroys its value as a basis for monopoly. The Electricity Boards are monopolists (sole suppliers), but oil and gas provide keen competition in the markets for industrial and domestic heating.

Tariffs provide another example of legal protection which, where the tariff is highly protective, might well lead to monopoly conditions in the home market.

c Control of factors of production

An effective monopoly may be established by controlling the supply of a factor of production. Trade unions attempt to exercise monopoly powers by virtue of their control over the supply of labour. The only really effective monopolies of this type, however, appear to have been established in the supply of minerals where sources are few and concentrated in clearly defined regions. China clay and nickel provide examples of raw materials the supplies of which are subject to monopoly or near-monopoly control. Similar conditions appear to apply in the case of diamonds.

d Control of selling outlets

A common method of establishing a monopoly situation has been to control the market outlets. A producer may buy a chain of shops (or public houses, or petrol stations) and restrict the sales from these outlets to his own products. He may, on the other hand, achieve similar results by operating a system of agencies whereby a distributor agrees to stock only the products of that firm, or group of firms, in return for which he is given an exclusive agency to supply such goods in his own area.

e Advertising

Advertising can be used as an effective barrier to entry. Where an industry comprises a few large firms selling well established brands supported by large scale advertising, it is extremely difficult for a new firm to break into the market. If we have, for example, an industry made up of three large firms each selling four brands, the initial advertising costs of trying to establish a new brand would be a formidable deterrent to any firm thinking of entering this market. A new entrant would be competing against twelve established brands rather than three existing firms.

f Agreements between producers

Adam Smith, in a frequently quoted passage, remarked, 'People of the same trade seldom meet together, even for merriment and diversion, but the conversation ends in conspiracy against the public, or on some contrivance to raise prices'. This might be held to be a rather harsh judgement, but there is plenty of evidence of the fact that, in many industries, producers have strongly exerted themselves to devise and operate schemes designed to restrict competition. Where such agreements are made, the individual firms retain their independence and freedom of action in all matters not covered by the agreement.

Such an agreement may take a variety of forms. It may be no more than an informal gentleman's agreement to collaborate in fixing prices or sharing markets: such informality does not imply ineffectiveness. More formal agreements are usually operated by a trade association, an organisation common to most industries and to which the majority of firms in that industry will belong. The fixing of common prices requires agreement between the firms concerned and must be derived, therefore, from some kind of average cost based upon the cost-structures of the member firms. The agreed price must not be so high as to tempt the low-cost producer to leave the association and sell at lower prices, nor so low as to leave no incentive for the higher-cost producers to join the scheme.

Agreements to maintain fixed prices and restrict output mean that the demand for any one firm's product will be very elastic at prices below the agreed price. This situation provides a great temptation for members to evade the restrictions by some form of 'hidden' price-cutting by, for example, raising the quality of the product, or by offering distributors better discounts or credit terms. It is, therefore, quite common for the rules of a trade association to set out in great detail the specification of the articles sold and the terms and conditions on which they are to be distributed.

3 The nature of restrictive trade practices

We now turn to a consideration of the types of business practice which have been used to establish, strengthen or exploit monopoly positions. It should be noted that the practices outlined are not normally operated in isolation, but rather as part of a general policy adopted by a monopoly. Only a limited selection of monopolistic practices is outlined in the following paragraphs.

a Exclusive dealing and collective boycott

These particular practices were found in the majority of the earlier investigations of the Monopolies Commission. Exclusive dealing refers to particular market arrangements whereby producers and distributors agree not to trade with non-parties to the agreement. Producers agree to supply their goods only to those distributors who are on the approved list, while the distributors agree not to stock the products of any 'outside' firms. The collective boycott is a means of enforcing such an agreement. Should any merchant break the agreement he will find that all the producers in the association will withhold their supplies. Arrangements such as these can be a very effective means of restricting the entry of new firms. If the majority of the market outlets are 'tied' to existing producers how can a new producer hope to market his product?

Exclusive dealing may be reinforced by the system of loyalty rebates. Under this system, distributors are encouraged to deal only with members of the producers' association by the offer of a substantial increase in their profit margins. They may, for example, be granted an extra 10% rebate on their purchases provided *all* their supplies are obtained from members of the producers' association.

b Control of materials, components and machinery

It is possible for a single firm, or group of firms, to exercise monopoly powers by virtue of their control over essential materials or components whereby supplies of such articles are withheld from independent firms. A firm supplying, say, oxygen might supply only those firms which agreed to use the oxygen plant which it also makes. A group of firms using some type of highly specialised machinery to make their goods might have an agreement with the machinery producers not to supply such machinery to potential rivals.

c Agreements on tendering

Many products are not made in anticipation of demand, but in response to a specific order. Such arrangements will apply, for example, in the civil engineering, shipbuilding and heavy electrical engineering industries. The normal procedure is for the buyer to invite tenders. Attempts to restrict competition in these circumstances would take the form of agreements between firms submitting tenders. Firms might, through their trade association, arrange to consult each other before submitting tenders, and, by agreeing on the prices to be quoted by each firm, organise some kind of market sharing.

d Quota schemes

There are several different quota schemes, but the basic principle is for members of the trade association to arrange to share out the market on some agreed basis. Each firm is allocated a quota which represents its share of the market for some agreed period of time. If the quota is expressed in *physical* terms it represents an extremely restrictive arrangement as it leaves the individual firm with no scope for expansion. There will be, in fact, a positive inducement for firms to indulge in take-over movements. The only way in which a member firm may increase its size is to take over another firm and hence absorb its quota. If the quota is calculated on a *percentage* basis then some incentive does exist for firms to expand the total market.

Normally such agreements contain provisions for financial penalties to be levied on firms exceeding their quotas, the revenue from such penalties providing compensation for those firms not reaching their agreed sales targets.

e Common prices

A most serious limitation on competition is the agreement by a number of firms to charge common prices. This is possible, of course, only where the article is of a fairly standardised character. Electric lamps, television tubes, electric cables, and building materials provide good examples of such products. It may be that the firms concerned are prepared to go much further than a simple agreement to charge common prices. They may agree to form a centralised selling agency to market the entire output of the group as a single seller. Profits are then distributed according to the individual firm's share of the market. This arrangement is known as a cartel.

f Resale price maintenance (RPM)

This practice will be discussed at greater length in a subsequent section, but we should note at this stage that RPM was, for many years, a most widespread restrictive practice. Under this scheme producers determine, and enforce, the prices at which their goods shall be sold at the wholesale and retail stages. They control, therefore, the gross profit margins at these stages, and hence rule out the possibility of price competition between the distributors of their products.

4 The extent of monopoly

It is only since the Monopolies Commission and the Restrictive Practices Court started their work that we have any substantial body of authoritative information on the extent of monopoly in British industry. Between the wars there were a number of official enquiries into various sectors of industry. The reports of these committees duly noted the increasing tendency towards large scale production and combination in industry, and drew attention to the possible dangers in some of the monopolistic tendencies. The problems of severe depression, however, overshadowed such issues. Indeed, the trade situation was so serious that the government of the day actually encouraged the formation of a number of cartels as a means of preserving capacity in certain important industries.

After the Second World War there were, again, a limited number of investigations into specific industries (e.g. Welsh slate, radio valves, cotton textile machinery, and building materials). Although finding considerable evidence of monopolistic practices, the committees often found that profits in such cases had not been excessive and there was no general call for legal prohibition or abolition of monopolies. Nevertheless there was sufficient evidence of such practices operating, or likely to operate against the public interest, to provoke demands for more thorough investigations and possibly some kind of government supervision.

Some evidence of the extent of concentration in British industry was provided by a report[1] by Messrs. Leak and Maizels published in 1945 and based on the 1935 *Census of Production*. It showed, for example, that in 70 of the trades studied, the degree of concentration was such that over 70% of the total employment was accounted for by the three largest firms. It also provided a list of over a hundred commodities produced by only one or two firms.

A similar type of study[2] by Messrs. Evely and Little produced similar concentration ratios for British industry in 1951. Their general summary stated the following: 'It appears that while there are only comparatively few trades with very strong monopolistic elements in their structure, it is also true that something approaching the perfectly competitive structure is only found in trades with about one-quarter of the total employment. By far the largest proportion of total employment is represented by the trades where conditions are suitable, or even favourable, for tacit or open collusion, or where the large units have, by virtue of their absolute size, considerable influence'.

[1] Leak and Maizels, *Journal of the Royal Statistical Society*, 1945.
[2] Evely and Little, *Concentration British Industry*, N.I.E.S.R.

3 THE BACKGROUND TO THE LEGISLATION

1 The case against monopoly

a Economic theory shows that, under monopoly conditions, output will be lower and prices will be higher than is the case under perfect competition. Output under perfect competition will be pushed to the level at which marginal cost equals price, but in a profit-maximising monopoly situation, output is restricted to the point where marginal revenue equals marginal cost. Since the monopolist faces a downward sloping demand curve, the marginal revenue curve will always be below the demand curve and the rising marginal cost curve must, therefore, cut the marginal revenue curve at a lower output (and therefore a higher price) than that which equates marginal cost and price.

b It follows, theoretically, from the above that the allocation of resources under monopoly is inferior to that provided by the competitive situation. Since, under perfect competition, price will be equal to marginal cost, the value to the community of the last unit of the commodity produced (i.e. price) will be exactly equal to the community's valuation of the resources used up in

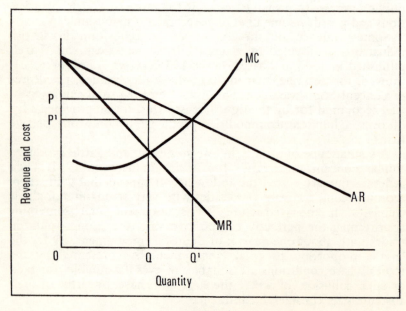

DIAGRAM 1

  i *Under monopoly conditions, Price = OP and Output = OQ*
 ii *In a competitive market, Price = OP¹ and Output = OQ¹*

producing that unit (i.e. marginal cost). Under monopoly, however, price exceeds marginal cost and consumers are paying more for the monopolist's output than is needed to purchase the factors of production required to produce that output. Consumers would, in fact, be prepared to buy further units of the product for a price exceeding the costs of production, but the monopolist's policy frustrates them.

c The monopolist, by virtue of his ability to restrict output, is able to earn abnormal profits. These surplus profits may be regarded as a redistribution of income away from consumers to the monopolist (and perhaps to his employees). The reader should check his understanding of these points by drawing the traditional diagram showing the output of the monopolist with abnormal profits, and by referring to *Understanding Economics* (S11).

d Economists have tended to take the view that monopolistic practices which tend to restrict the entry of new firms are unfair and harmful. They create rigidities in the structure of industry and they provide a brake on the pace of innovation. It is held that the monopolist, insulated from the pressure of competitors, has much less incentive to develop new techniques and new products than has the firm operating in highly competitive markets.

These criticisms of monopoly, of course, are based on the view that perfect competition provides the 'best' allocation of resources. But this particular view depends upon many assumptions, some of which may appear to be very unrealistic. It depends also, for example, on one's view of the present distribution of income. Perfect competition will lead to a pattern of resource allocation which is determined by the free choices of consumers exercised in the market place. The pattern of consumer demand, however, will reflect the existing distribution of income and, if this is considered to be 'unsatisfactory', then it will obviously lead to a pattern of resource allocation which is also 'unsatisfactory'.

The preceding arguments against monopoly also assume that the marginal cost curve of the monopolist is identical with the total supply curve of the competitive industry. This is not very likely and it can be shown that it is possible for the monopolist to achieve economies of scale which might well produce a monopoly price lower than the competitive price (see diagram 2).

2 Arguments in favour of monopoly

a We have already noted how many modern developments in technology have made possible some very important economies of scale.

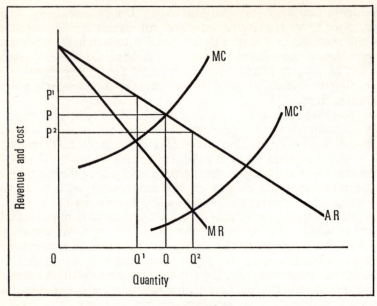

DIAGRAM 2

i   *In a competitive market, Price = OP and Output = OQ*
ii   *Industry becomes monopolised, Price = OP^1 and Output = OQ^1*
iii   *Monopolisation of industry makes possible economies of scale, Price = OP^2 and Output = OQ^2*

This is, of course, an argument for the large firm rather than for monopoly, but it is becoming increasingly the case that a market may be supplied, at the lowest possible cost, by a single firm or by an oligopoly. If a competitive industry were to be monopolised it is not very likely that the cost conditions would remain the same — economies of scale would almost certainly mean lower cost curves.

Low costs do not necessarily mean low prices — they may mean higher profits, and this is one of the reasons why certain industries have been nationalised. While nationalisation, of itself, cannot ensure greater efficiency or lower prices, it could be a means of preventing abuses of monopoly power.

b   One argument put forward for monopoly is that competition is not conducive to technical progress in the form of new inventions and improved techniques. Introducing a new product is a risky undertaking and the development process is often very costly. Firms are much more likely to undertake such projects, it is said, where their markets are protected. Again, technical progress in many industries requires costly research and development and such resources are more likely to be provided under monopoly than under perfect competition. These arguments are summarised in the phrase 'only the secure can afford to be venturesome'. To give further emphasis to this argument it should be noted that the monopolist does have an incentive to reduce costs since he will benefit, in the long term, from the greater profits. Under competition, however, the incentive will be less since the greater profits will represent only short-term gains.

c Where an industry is affected by a downward shift in demand requiring structural changes, it is likely that a planned reduction of capacity will cause less hardship and be more efficient than the adjustments brought about by the competitive process. Competition will bring about the necessary structural changes but the process is likely to be protracted − savage price cutting at the expense of adequate depreciation allowances will probably lead to an excessive number of firms all working below capacity (i.e. short-time working), usually with out of date machinery. The industry has been reduced, but not in a way which increases its efficiency. It was this type of situation which caused the government to encourage the setting up of monopolistic organisations in the 1930s. Where there is some degree of unified control over the industry a reduction of capacity can take the form of closures of the least efficient plants and a concentration of production in the more efficient units.

d One of the great weaknesses of perfect competition, or situations where there are relatively large numbers of competing firms, is the danger of over-reaction to shifts in demand. An increase in demand where supply is fairly inelastic, will lead to a considerable rise in price. Each producer raises his production target for the succeeding period, anxious to benefit from the higher prices, but tending to ignore the fact that other producers are doing likewise. When these plans mature there is likely to be an excess of supply over demand at the new price. Prices will now fall sharply and this will lead once again to over-compensation by producers in the opposite direction. If demand is fairly unstable there will be continuous swings around the equilibrium price.

A monopolist, since he is the sole producer, should not make the same mistakes. He is responsible for meeting the total demand for the product and should be more aware of market changes and more capable of making effective adjustments of output than the individual firm under competitive conditions. In other words a monopoly situation should give a much greater degree of price stability than is likely under perfect competition. This particular argument provides one of the reasons for government initiative in sponsoring the agricultural marketing boards which are cartel-type organisations.

4 THE DEVELOPMENT OF
PUBLIC POLICY ON MONOPOLY

It is now generally accepted that it is the responsibility of the state to minimise any waste of resources due to inefficiency, to prevent the exploitation of weaker parties in exchange transactions, and to ensure that the more powerful competing interests do not eliminate their weaker opponents simply to acquire monopoly positions. In order to achieve these ends the state may adopt one or more of several possible policies.

It may, for example prohibit restrictive agreements which are intended to establish monopoly power. This dogmatic approach wishes to see what is called 'fair' competition applying everywhere and its application is seen in the early American legislation on monopolies — the Sherman Act of 1890 and the Clayton Act of 1914. It aims not at regulating monopoly, but at preventing its development.

A second type of policy is more pragmatic and recognises that in certain situations, for example in the field of public utilities, monopoly is probably the most efficient type of organisation. The appropriate policy in this case will not be the breaking up of the monopoly, but the provision of some means of ensuring that the monopoly power will not be used against the public interest. In Britain, the state has for a long time exercised this type of regulation, and there is a long history of state control over the operations and pricing policies of the railways. The same was true of the privately-owned utilities supplying gas, electricity and water. Later on, of course, the regulation of private ownership in these industries was replaced by public ownership.

A third type of policy carries the principle of acceptance much further and allows that monopolistic organisations may be justified in areas other than those in which monopoly seems 'natural'. It is more concerned with business practices which have monopolistic motives, and is prepared to assess these on their individual merits rather than invoke general prohibition. Recent British legislation is based upon this third type of policy.

Although, at common law, contracts in restraint of trade have for centuries been unenforceable, this meant very little in practice. Although such contracts could not be enforced in the law-courts if broken — since judges would refuse to compel those who were parties to them to behave contrary to the public interest — yet they clearly could not be forbidden either, since as long as the firms making them were satisfied with the arrangements and honoured them, no one was likely to make a complaint.

Special statutory powers were required to accomplish this

object, but British legislation in this field came relatively late. One reason for this may be that down to 1932, the prevalence of free trade severely limited the power of domestic monopolies. As we have seen, however, there was considerable evidence both before and after the Second World War that monopolistic tendencies were widespread and increasing. The first real hint that the government meant to act came in the 1944 White Paper on Employment Policy which, in one passage, stated, 'The government will therefore seek powers to inform themselves of the extent and effect of restrictive agreements and of the activities of combines; and to take appropriate action to check practices which may bring advantages to sectional producing interests but work to the detriment of the country as a whole'.

Legislation followed in 1948.

1 The Monopolies and Restrictive Practices Act 1948.

This legislation gave expression to the government's view that monopolies and restrictive practices were not bad in themselves, but, nevertheless, they had the power to operate against the public interest. There was, therefore, a strong case for investigation in order to determine whether such agreements were operating to raise prices, to restrict the growth of new firms, to reduce output, and to delay the introduction of new tehniques.

a The Monopolies and Restrictive Practices Commission

The Act provided for the establishment of a Monopolies Commission which was to be a small body of not less than four and not more than ten members. The idea was for the Commission to work as a group and to build up by experience, a body of uniform criteria and principles. The duties of the Commission were to investigate, report, and make recommendations on situations referred to it by the Board of Trade.[1] The Commission had no power to initiate investigations and could only take action after a reference had been made. The government was under no obligation to act on the recommendations made by the Commission.

The conditions to which the Act applied were the fields of supply, processing and export of goods, where one-third of the goods in question were supplied in the British Isles (or any substantial part thereof) by or to any one person, or group of persons, acting in such a way as to restrict competition. The Board of Trade could also ask the Commission to examine the effect on the public interest of certain specified business practices.

While the Commission was given full powers to call for evidence from firms and individuals during its investigation, it had no powers to give effect to its recommendations. The Board of Trade was placed under an obligation to publish the reports of the Commission, and where the Commission found that monopoly powers existed and were operating against the public interest, the government could make an order declaring the arrangements unlawful and obliging the parties to such arrangements to bring them to an end.

b The work of the Commission

It was intended that the Commission should function as an independent body free from political interference so that it would acquire the reputation of an independent tribunal. Its membership

[1] This responsibility is now exercised by the Department of Trade and Industry.

was to be broadly based, with members drawn from the Civil Service, industry, commerce, the law, the professions, the trade unions and the academic world.

In the early years, the time taken to produce the reports was subject to considerable criticism. The first report, on dental goods, took twenty months to prepare. Although the reports were acknowledged to be very sound (and, for the first time, provided detailed and authoritative accounts of the structure of British industry), it was held by many critics, that they were too long and too few. This criticism led to an Act of Parliament in 1953 which enlarged the maximum membership of the Commission of twenty-five, enabling it to work in two or more groups and to conduct a number of investigations at the same time.

c The reports

Most of the reports tend to be lengthy and contain a great deal of factual information of great interest to economists. It is strongly recommended that students look at one or two of these reports in order to get a clearer picture of the work of the Monopolies Commission.

The reports usually begin with a general view of the industry concerned, and provide details of the historical development of the industry up to the time of the investigation. Then follows a section dealing with the existing arrangements in the industry. In its earlier reports the Commission found considerable evidence of the widespread application of monopolistic practices. Exclusive dealing and collective boycott were found in fifteen of the first twenty cases while some kind of arrangement to fix prices at a common level were found in sixteen of the twenty. Collective resale price maintenance, restrictive agreements on the supply of machinery and components, loyalty rebates, and quota schemes were also found to be common practices.

A further section of each report deals with the structure of costs, prices and profits in the industry. Here the Commission has the difficult task of deciding what is a 'reasonable' price and what are 'reasonable' profits. These terms cannot be defined accurately, but have to be judged in the light of such factors as the effectiveness of any restrictive practices employed, the attainable levels of efficiency, the degree of protection afforded by tariffs, the extent of any necessary and costly research, the desirable scale of production and the requirements for future investment. In several industries the Commission have thought the levels of profits to be unjustifiably high.

A final section of the report sets out the Commission's conclusions and recommendations. One of the great problems facing the Commission is that of interpreting the term 'in the public interest'. The 1948 Act did attempt to produce some guide lines by indicating the following criteria: 'the production, treatment and distribution of goods by the most efficient and economic means, in such volume and at such prices as will best meet the requirements of home and overseas markets; the organisation of industry and trade in such a way that their efficiency is progressively increased and new enterprise is encouraged; the fullest use and best distribution of men, materials and industrial capacity; the development of technical improvement and the expansion of existing markets and the opening up of new ones'. To these the Commission have added other guiding principles — for example, the individual entrepreneur should be free to enter the trade of his choosing.

The Commission is well aware of the theoretical arguments favouring competition (lower costs and prices and the ready response of producers to changing consumer preferences), but it has to weigh these against arguments presented by the industrialists in favour of certain restrictive practices. These practices, it has been claimed, result in more stable trading conditions, fair prices to consumers, ensure better standards of quality and service, encourage efficiency by the exchange of technical information and provide safeguards against damaging price wars.

One of the tasks facing the Commission is that of assessing the total effect of a number of restrictive practices and estimating whether there is any net benefit. In the investigation into the supply of electric lamps, it accepted the practice of manufacturers in fixing common selling prices because it believed that the agreement facilitated technical co-operation between producers which led to lower costs of production. In its report on the supply of linoleum, the Commission accepted the common price system because it maintained a stability of prices in a situation where raw material prices fluctuated and this meant that distributors were prepared to hold larger stocks. Where there is a situation of fluctuating prices, distributors will be very reluctant to order and hold large stocks since they will be at a disadvantage if prices fall shortly after placing a large order.

Although the Commission was prepared to leave existing arrangements undisturbed in certain circumstances, its conclusions generally indicated that restrictions on competition were harmful, since they tended to make for rigidity in industrial structure and to impede innovation and expansion.

Over the years, the Monopolies Commission has made a variety of recommendations for the control or modification of the policies of different firms. These have included proposals for, price reductions; government supervision of prices, costs and profits; reductions in advertising and other selling costs; the lowering of tariffs on competing imports, and the prohibition of any further take-overs of competitors.

d Government action

In general, the government has preferred to implement its decisions by means of negotiated agreements rather than use its powers to make statutory orders. In most cases these negotiations have ended with the Department of Trade and Industry receiving and accepting assurances that the firms concerned will abandon or modify the offending practices.

Between 1948 and 1956 the Commission produced twenty reports on individual industries and a further report that had a more general reference. The latter report had great significance. The Commission had been asked to undertake an investigation into practices which came under the general heading of 'collective discrimination'. The practices in question were those where 'agreements between two or more persons required them to withhold goods from any persons named or defined in the agreement, or requiring them to supply such persons on less favourable terms than others' (e.g. exclusive dealing, collective boycott, and loyalty rebates). Here the Commission was not restricted to one industry; its instructions were to look at the whole field and examine such practices wherever they were found. It was discovered that in fact they were very widely in operation. The report it presented in 1955 contained a majority and a minority recommendation. The majority of the Commission recommended that such practices should be made illegal while the minority recommended that all such practices should be registered and investigated individually. The report led to legislation in 1956.

2 The Restrictive Trade Practices Act 1956

The 1956 Act was divided into three principal parts. Part I provided for the registration of restrictive trade practices and for their judicial investigation by a court of law. The government did not accept the Monopolies Commission recommendation for a legal prohibition of these practices. Part II dealt with resale price maintenance and Part III reconstituted the Monopolies Commission and amended its functions.

Part I. Registration and investigation of restrictive trade agreements

The restrictive agreements with which the Act was concerned were those between 'persons carrying on business as producers, processors, or suppliers of goods . . . or associations of such persons, under which mutual restrictions are accepted in the matter of prices, terms and conditions of trading, quantities or descriptions of goods, processes of manufacture, areas or places of trading, and persons with whom business is done'.

The Act provided for the appointment of a Registrar of restrictive trade agreements, the establishment of a register of such agreements, and the creation of a Restrictive Practices Court. The registration of such agreements was made compulsory and the Registrar's duties were to keep the register, decide the order in which cases shall be heard by the Court, to ensure that the interests of third parties were fully considered and to express the public interest during the hearings of the Court. All agreements registered were assumed, on the face of it, to be against the public interest. The onus was upon the parties to the agreement to show that they were not acting contrary to the public interest.

The Restrictive Practices Court has the powers, rights, privileges, and authority of the High Court. Its decisions become the law of the land. It consists of five judges and not more than ten laymen whose function it is to advise the judges on matters of business practice. The Court may sit in several divisions, each division consisting of not less than one judge and two other members.

The procedure of the Court is clearly defined. Parties to restrictive trading agreements must demonstrate to the Court's satisfaction that their agreements (a) satisfy one or more of seven defined circumstances (the seven gateways) and (b) are not unreasonable, having regard to the balance between these circumstances (i.e. the gateways) and any detriment to the public, or to persons not party to the agreement, resulting from the operation of the agreement. A restrictive practice, therefore, has to jump two hurdles in order to be declared not contrary to the public interest.

The 'seven gateways' are as follows:[1]

a the restriction must be reasonably necessary in order to protect the public against injury (e.g. drugs and medicines might be supplied only by qualified and registered pharmacist);

b the removal of the restriction must deny to the public other specific and substantial benefits enjoyed or likely to be enjoyed by them as a result of the restriction (e.g. a common price agreement might lead to technical collaboration between firms which leads to greater efficiency and more standardisation);

c the restriction must be necessary to counter restrictive

---

[1] The 1968 Act has introduced a new 'gateway'.

measures taken by any one person not party to the agreement;

   d   the restriction must be necessary to enable parties to the agreement to negotiate fair terms with buyers or sellers who control a preponderant part of the trade (e.g. where there are a number of competing firms facing a monopsonist);

   e   the removal of the restriction must lead to serious and persistent unemployment in an area which is heavily dependent upon the particular industry;

   f   the restriction must be necessary in order to maintain the volume or earnings of the export trade where this is substantial in relation to the export trade of the United Kingdom as a whole, or in relation to the whole business of that trade or industry (e.g. a restriction of price competition might encourage firms to embark upon joint advertising, market research, and other selling projects in overseas markets);

   g   the restriction must be required to maintain some other restriction which the Court has found to be justified.

About 3000 agreements have been placed on the register, of which about three-quarters contain price restrictions and four-fifths are between manufacturers. About two-thirds of the agreements have been terminated without reference to the Court. These agreements were either voluntarily abandoned or modified so that they did not come within the law. Something like 625 have been referred to the Court, but, again, many were abandoned before hearing and only 390 cases have proceeded to judgement by the Court. Of the latter, 46 were defended, but only 11 were approved by the Court. It has, therefore, proved extremely difficult to obtain the Court's approval of a restrictive agreement.

The number of cases heard by the Court has not been very great, but, by carefully selecting the cases to be heard, the Registrar was able to make each case an important test case for a number of similar agreements. If a particular case is lost, it is most likely that a large number of similar agreements will be abandoned. In fact, the number of agreements found to be consistent with the public interest amounts to less than 1 per cent of the *registered* agreements. It is difficult to judge the full impact of the legislation because we do not know how many associations chose to abandon agreements rather than submit them to registration. There is no doubt, however, that the policy has removed a great mass of price-fixing arrangements which existed prior to 1956. The Registrar has reported that no cases of real significance remain to be dealt with.

Some of the Court's decisions have surprised the pundits. In the case of the Yarn Spinners' Agreement, the respondents[1] proved to

---

[1] i.e. the parties refuting the arguments that their restrictive practices are operating against the public interest.

the satisfaction of the Court that the termination of the agreement would lead to serious and persistent unemployment (gateway e), yet the agreement was found to be contrary to the public interest because the second hurdle was not cleared. The Court decided that the detriments in the form of higher consumer prices, the loss of exports due to higher prices, and the waste of resources due to excess capacity, exceeded the benefits.

In the case of the Black Nut and Bolts Agreement, the Court decided that the price-fixing agreement was not contrary to the public interest because it led to a stability of prices and it meant that buyers were not put to the trouble of 'shopping around'. The additional cost of discovering which manufacturers were charging the lowest prices was expected to be greater than the savings achieved by buying at the lowest free market price.

On the effects of ending restrictive agreements the Registrar has commented that, in some industries, competition soon appears, bringing benefits to consumers and increasing efficiency in industries supplying materials and components as a result of the keener buying. In other industries, particularly the stable or slowly expanding ones, the ending of agreements appears to have little effect at first, but in some of these cases there is evidence of a revival of price competition. The Registrar has expressed concern that the passing of the Act has led to the widespread substitution of 'open price agreements' for the registrable type of agreement. The parties to such agreements undertake to give each other advance information of the changes they propose to make in their pricing policies. Such agreements could operate in ways which restrict competition.

Part II. Resale Price Maintenance
The second section of the 1956 Act dealt with the practice of resale price maintenance. Collective resale price maintenance under which producers collectively enforce their retail prices was declared illegal. Individual resale price maintenance, on the other hand, was made legally enforceable, and for the first time a producer could now use the courts of law to enforce the fixed wholesale and retail prices of his own products.

Part III. The Monopolies Commission
The third section of the 1956 Act reduced the Monopolies Commission from twenty-five to ten members and no longer permitted it to work in groups. Its role was restricted to monopoly situations where a single firm is responsible for one-third or more of the total supply (i.e. unified monopolies or oligopolies), and to the investigation of restrictive practices which related exclusively to the export trade.

3 The Resale Prices Act 1964

In the post-war period there has been a growing controversy over the merits and demerits of RPM. To some extent this has been due to the continuing problem of inflation which has focused attention on the subject of retail prices. The arguments for and against RPM have become widely known.

RPM, it is said, benefits the consumer in that he is not subject to the frustrating time-consuming task of searching for the outlets selling at the lowest prices. Since uniform prices appear to indicate uniform quality, he feels confident that he is getting what he thinks he is paying for. Price-cutting, it is held, will lead to quality-cutting, and price competition at the retail stage will cause shopkeepers to concentrate on the fast moving popular lines thus reducing the variety of goods available to the public. Under RPM retailers are forced to compete by providing services in the form of after-sales service, free delivery, better quality retail outlets and so on. These services, the supporters of RPM hold, greatly benefit the consumer. He also benefits, they maintain, from the large number of retail outlets which the system encourages, since producers fix retail profit margins at generous levels which allow less efficient firms to survive.

On the other hand, it is argued that RPM greatly restricts the freedom of choice of the consumer. He cannot choose between a lower-priced product supplied without any of the services mentioned above and the higher-priced product supplied with a variety of services. The practice of RPM enables the less efficient retailers to remain in business since their more efficient rivals cannot eliminate them by using the weapon of price competition. This gives rise to a multiplicity of retail outlets operating under conditions of excess capacity. Briefly, RPM, its critics claim, subsidises the less efficient, raises costs, and maintains prices at artificially high levels.

The case against RPM seemed to be gaining ground and the provision in the 1956 Act which provided for judicial enforcement of individual RPM came as a surprise to many commentators. In the years following the 1956 legislation, several developments caused the government to think again and, eventually, to change its policy. The retail trade in the 1950s and 1960s was undergoing some major structural changes. The multiples[1] were steadily increasing their share of the markets and horizontal integration was producing some very large retail combines, particularly in furniture, electrical goods, clothing and footwear. Supermarkets were beginning to make their appearance and new technologies in

[1] Large retail firms with many branches.

food preparation, packaging and stock control were being applied to yield great economies of scale. The forces of competition were becoming stronger and RPM was increasingly seen as a barrier to the expansion of the more efficient firms. It was already being evaded by a variety of techniques. Artificially inflated trade-in values, the growing use of trading stamps, and the use of distributors' own brand names were the most common of the practices designed to escape from the strait jacket of RPM. The government eventually recognised and accepted the fact that RPM was largely discredited and passed the Resale Prices Act in 1964.

This Act, passed in July 1964, made all forms of RPM illegal except for those which passed the scrutiny of the Restrictive Practices Court. The procedure for dealing with RPM is very similar to that laid down in the 1956 Act. All agreements have to be registered and are then subject to investigation by the Court. Those agreements not placed on the register by the closing date (16th November 1964) were deemed to be illegal. Firms which registered their agreements were allowed to continue enforcement of RPM until their application was heard by the Court.

As in the 1956 Act, the claims for exemption had to satisfy certain defined conditions. In this case firms or trade associations could choose one or more of five gateways by claiming that the abandonment of the agreement would:

  a reduce the quality or variety of the goods on sale;
  b substantially reduce the number of shops in which the goods were sold;
  c lead to increased prices in the long run;
  d cause the goods to be sold under conditions which would cause danger to health;
  e cause after-sales services to cease, or be substantially reduced.

If the respondents satisfied the Court on one or more of these conditions they would still have to clear the second hurdle. This was the same as that defined in the 1956 Act — the benefits to the public alleged to accrue from RPM had to outweigh the benefits to be obtained from its abolition.

When the registration period expired some 700 applications for exemption had been recorded. These covered about 500 classes of goods. It was noteworthy that no applications for exemption had been received from important industries such as motor-cars and accessories, paints, wallpaper and sports goods. Some larger firms such as ICI, Dunlop, Gillette and Distillers had abandoned RPM even before its legal prohibition. In view of these developments the Registrar anticipated, correctly as it happened, that very few of the cases would be contested and the majority voluntarily abandoned before the cases came up for hearing. Where no defence is offered the Registrar asks the Court to make an order to the effect that the goods are no longer exempt from the general ban on RPM.

The first case to be heard was that of the Chocolate and Confectionery manufacturers, and the Court ruled, in July 1967, that RPM in confectionery was illegal. This decision undoubtedly discouraged many firms from defending RPM. In June 1968 the Footwear Manufacturers lost their case, a decision which caused further voluntary abandonment of RPM agreements. The situation in February 1970 was that only two categories of product were still subject to RPM, proprietary medicines and books. The Court ruled in favour of RPM on books in 1962, and in favour of RPM on proprietary medicines in June 1970.

In a review of the first four years following the official ending of RPM, *The Economist* (29.3.69) noted that although there had been no flood of price cutting and hoards of small shopkeepers had not, as feared, been driven out of business, there have been significant developments. Price cutting has appeared, most notably in the grocery trade. Severe competition in the sale of wines and spirits, electrical goods and tobacco has reduced prices substantially, but in the case of some consumer goods (e.g. furniture, watches and clocks, stationery and toys) there has been very little change. The end of RPM does not appear to have had much effect on indirect price competition; 'special offers' and trading stamps are still flourishing. The number of shops has fallen, but RPM is only one factor in this decline — other features such as the Selective Employment Tax, the trend to larger shops and tougher economic conditions were also contributory factors in this change in the structure of retailing.

4 The Monopolies and Mergers Act 1965

After several years of experience of operating the 1956 Act it was being argued that one effect of the legislation on restrictive agreements has been to promote mergers. Integration, both vertical and horizontal, can be an effective way of escaping the surveillance of the Court (although it could lead to investigation by the Commission). A restrictive agreement might be replaced by a merger. The growing tide of take-over bids led to attention once again becoming concentrated on the dominant firm. Commentators were also drawing attention to the fact that service industries — an increasingly important sector of the economy — were outside the scope of the legislation on monopolies. Both of these important matters were dealt with in the 1965 Monopolies and Mergers Act.

The 1965 Act, in effect, restored the 1953 structure of the

Monopolies Commission by increasing its maximum size to twenty-five and restoring its right to work in groups. The Commission's work was substantially extended by including in its terms of reference the right to investigate monopoly situations and restrictive agreements in the service industries. The major innovation in this legislation, however, was the power to refer proposed mergers for investigation by the Monopolies Commission. The Act applies to cases where the proposed merger involves the take-over of gross assets in excess of £5m, or where it would create or intensify a monopoly. It is for the Department of Trade and Industry to decide which mergers should be referred to the Commission, which must report within six months of any such reference (nine months in special cases). If the merger is found to be against the public interest, the Department of Trade and Industry may prohibit it, or dissolve it if it has already taken place. Special conditions apply to mergers in the newspaper world. The Act makes it illegal for one newspaper to merge with another where the combined average daily circumulation exceeds 500 000 copies, without permission of the Department of Trade and Industry.

Since the Act was passed a large number of mergers have been considered by the Department of Trade and Industry, but only a very small percentage have been referred to the Commission (only 9 out of the first 170). There have been relatively few cases where mergers have been declared contrary to the public interest. Such decisions have attracted much attention and a fair amount of criticism. The Commission blocked a proposed merger between the multiple tailors Montague Burton and United Drapery Stores on the grounds that it would lead to a substantial contraction of competition in retailing and a concentration of buying power which might adversely affect the wollen industry. A proposed merger between Associated Fisheries and the Ross Group was rejected because it would lead to too great a concentration of power in trawler fishing and in distribution. More recently a proposed merger between Ranks and De la Rue was rejected on the grounds that management difficulties would be likely to develop (De la Rue executives were unwilling parties) and because it was feared that important trading links with the USA would be adversely affected.

Critics have pointed to some inconsistencies. In the proposed merger between Burtons and United Draperies the joint market share in men's suits would have been 36 per cent, yet, in the report on Pilkingtons, a market share of 91 per cent was not considered objectionable. The union between the National Provincial and Westminster banks was approved while the proposed merger between Midland and Barclays was not supported. It has also been pointed out monopolies much more formidable than some of those rejected, have been allowed through without reference to the Commission e.g. GEC/AEI/English Electric.

For a period (1966–1970) the official policy on mergers was confused by the existence of a government-sponsored agency, the *Industrial Reorganisation Corporation.*[1] The IRC's task was to encourage restructuring and regrouping of industries in which such developments would lead to greater efficiency. For this purpose it was supplied with public funds which it could invest in approved projects. The organisation was active in promoting some important mergers e.g. GEC/AEI, and British Leyland. Many people took the view that the IRC and the Monopolies Commission were pursuing conflicting objectives. This was not necessarily so, because the official policy is aimed at the removal of the disadvantages of monopoly rather than the complete elimination of monopoly. Current thinking on the topic of mergers is much concerned with the problem of conglomerates and the subject is discussed later in this chapter.

5 The Restrictive Practices Act 1968

The general purpose of this Act was to amend Part 1 of the 1956 Act so as to make its operation more flexible and to improve its enforcement. The main provisions are set out below.

a. The Department of Trade and Industry is given authority to exempt certain restrictive agreements from registration. To be eligible for such exemption an agreement must be calculated to promote the carrying out of an industrial or commercial project of substantial importance to the economy (discussed below).

b. Ministers in charge of appropriate departments are given power to exempt from registration any agreements made in support of a prices and incomes policy.

c. The exemption procedure is also available in relation to agreements which relate to standards of dimension, design or quality of goods. (e.g. an agreement not to sell goods which do not conform with a relevant British Standard)

d. The Secretary of State for Trade and Industry is given power to make an order calling up for registration any class of information agreements falling within the definition given in the Act.

e. The Act introduces a new 'gateway' into the provisions of the 1956 Act, by which a restriction may be held not to be contrary to the public interest so long as it does not directly or indirectly discourage competition. This provides a possible defence for information agreements.

[1] The I.R.C. was wound up in 1971.

There appear to be good reasons for the provisions in section (a). The government is now prepared to endorse certain restrictive agreements where they can be shown to operate in the national interest. For example, it has been demonstrated that certain industries could bring about a substantial saving on the country's import bill by creating capacity within this country to produce materials which are, at present, being bought abroad. But who is to build the plant? The company concerned must be certain of a market large enough to justify the investment. But this can only be achieved by the kind of agreement whereby Company A agrees not to manufacture a certain product in order to leave Company B a market large enough to justify its investment and to make its cost internationally competitive. Perhaps Company B is able to return the compliment by accepting some other restriction. British markets may be too small to act as a base for producers of goods which are in competition with overseas giants. The British machine tool industry has been cited as an example. The IRC pointed out that competition between British companies often works to the advantage of better organised overseas competitors and what was needed, it thought, was a greater rationalisation of product ranges (i.e. a greater degree of product specialisation as between firms). The kind of changes proposed in these examples call for a type of market-sharing agreement which the 1956 Act was expressly designed to forbid; hence this exemption provision in the 1968 legislation.

Section (d) refers to the 'open price' agreements mentioned earlier. The breaking of a restrictive agreement has sometimes been followed by the substitution of an 'open price' or *Information agreement* whereby the firms in an industry agree to supply each other with information on their pricing and marketing policies. It is strongly felt by many observers that such agreements may be used as a means of avoiding competition. In 1969 the Secretary of State ordered that such agreements should be registrable.

6 The Fair Trading Act 1973

This very important legislation brought about substantial changes in the machinery for the control of monopolistic practices. It has created a centralised organisation for the supervision and monitoring of the whole field of competition in the private sector of the economy together with some limited powers for investigating the public sector. The main provisions of the Act are,

i. the setting up of a new body, the office of the Director-General of Fair Trading,

ii. the Monopolies Commission is renamed the Monopolies and Mergers Commission and given wider powers of enquiry, and

iii. the criterion for a monopoly situation is reduced from one-third (minimum) market share to a one-quarter market share.

The Director-General of Fair Trading

The holder of this office is given wide ranging powers extending beyond the responsibility for carrying out monopoly policy. He has the responsibility for maintaining a continuous review of consumer trade practices and commercial activities. Acting upon information received from official bodies or consumers he can initiate investigations into business practices and any 'unfair' practices will be reported to a Consumer Protection Advisory Committee. If the Committee is in agreement, the Director-General can recommend action to the Secretary of State who has powers to make a 'cease and desist' order. The types of 'unfair' practices from which the consumer is to be given protection are those which,

i. mislead consumers about the nature, quality or quantity of goods involved in a transaction,

ii. mislead, or withhold adequate information from consumers about their rights and obligations under a transaction,

iii. subject consumers to undue pressure, and

iv. cause the terms or conditions of a transaction to be so adverse as to be inequitable.

In addition to his role as a consumers' watchdog, the Director-General of Fair Trading is responsible for the implementation of the government's policy on monopolies and mergers.

He has power to make references to the Monopolies and Mergers Commission (although he can be overruled by the Secretary of State). He cannot refer mergers or the nationalised industries to the Commission − this is the responsibility of the appropriate Minister − but he is responsible for carrying out the preliminary work in assessing monopoly situations and merger proposals.

The Director-General has taken over the duties formerly carried out by the Registrar of Restrictive Agreements. He has the tasks of keeping the register and making references to the Restrictive Practices Court.

In effect, the Fair Trading Office will become a central source of information and advice for Ministers on consumer protection, monopoly, mergers and restrictive practices, as well as a centre for initiating public action in these fields.

The Monopolies and Mergers Commission

The Monopolies and Mergers Commission will continue to function in much the same way as before the Act, but its role has been extended and modified. It is given power to investigate the nationalised industries, and for the first time local (geographical) monopolies are subject to its scrutiny. As a means of speeding up the Commission's procedures, the Secretary of State for Trade and Industry can set a time limit on the Commission's enquiries, and, if necessary, the Commission can be asked to restrict its investigation to some particular aspect of a monopoly or merger. The Commission is newly empowered to look at the restrictive practices in the labour markets, but these will be 'study' enquiries only with no provision for any ministerial action.

The criterion for a monopoly situation is reduced from a one-third market share to a one-quarter share. For merger references the criteria are (a) where the market share resulting from the merger is at least one-quarter of the total market, or (b) where the value of the assets taken over exceeds £5 million (the same as previously).

The Public Interest

One interesting feature of the 1973 Act is that it attempts to provide more guidance to the investigators on the subject of the public interest. A new definition contained in the Act includes such phrases as, 'the desirability of maintaining and promoting effective competition'; 'the need for promoting through competition, the reduction of costs, and the development of new techniques and new products, . . . and facilitating the entry of new competitors into existing markets'. The emphasis is much more on competition. The 1948 Act did not specifically mention 'competition' among the public interest criteria. Nevertheless, the 1973 legislation clearly lays down that 'all matters which appear relevant must be considered', and makes particular mention of the need to maintain a balanced distribution of industry and employment in the UK. The aim of promoting competition, while being given much more prominence, will not be the overriding consideration. An increase in monopoly power (e.g. by merger) which, it is believed, would substantially improve employment prospects in, say, a development area, might well be judged to be in the public interest.

6 THE CURRENT SITUATION

It is hoped that the creation of an office with continuing responsibility for examining defects in market structure and conduct over the entire range of economic activities will be a powerful means of improving what is officially described as 'competition policy'. The Director-General of Fair Trading with the increased staff and resources at his disposal will be able to carry out more detailed and systematic preliminary enquiries so that issues of real importance are given priority when references are made to the Monopolies and Mergers Commission.

On the other hand, critics point to the fact that the policy still lacks a clearly defined objective. The strengthening of competition is now a stated aim of policy, but the alternative objectives of maintaining local employment opportunities and redistributing industry may lead to different and sometimes contrary conclusions.

The issue which is probably causing most discussion at the present time is the official line on mergers and more especially the problems of *conglomerates*. A conglomerate is a multiproduct firm, often the result of both vertical and horizontal integration, which embraces firms operating in several different industries. Although it may be an extremely large firm, it may be outside the scope of the law on monopolies, because it does not control one-quarter of the market in any one of its activities. It may be that one of the reasons why the critical market share was reduced from one-third to one-quarter in the 1973 Act, was to bring more of these firms into the orbit of the Monopolies and Mergers Commission. Conglomerates may represent important concentrations of economic power, but at the same time, they may be no more than loose aggregates of small and medium sized companies each of which is below the optimum size for its particular activity. Just the sort of company, in fact, which the IRC had tried to prod into larger groups within an industry. Once a company becomes part of a conglomerate, it could be very difficult to prise it out in order to form part of a rationalisation programme for a given type of industrial activity. It would be very difficult to rationalise, say, the machine tool industry if the majority of firms were members of conglomerates. It has been argued that many of these conglomerates are too diversified and fail to achieve the full potential economies of scale in any of their many lines of activity.

Relatively few mergers are referred to the Commission and of those referred about one half have been approved. The business world is not so much interested in the number of references to the Monopolies and Merger Commission, but in what criteria the

Commission applies. The Minister for Trade and Consumer Affairs stated in November 1973[1] that 'the government believes that competition policy should generally be in favour of more competition rather than less'. Important horizontal mergers, therefore, are likely to be referred, but it is difficult to know how much weight the Department of Trade and Industry will attach to countervailing factors where firms might no longer be capable of surviving on their own, or where there are strong arguments for larger size in relation to efficiency and employment. In the case of conglomerates it is extremely difficult to produce guide lines, and much more study needs to be done on the economic and social consequences of this type of merger.

The Commission will also have to take account of the fact that Britain is now competing in the larger European market. This is not necessarily an argument for more mergers. Economists have found that an industry's ability to compete in the E.E.C. is related much more to superior plant and techniques than to company size. Entry into the E.E.C., of course, has made British industry subject to the regulations of the Community and legislation currently proposed would give the European Commission wide ranging powers to control mergers in all industries and not just in coal and steel as at present.

[1] In the same statement he indicated that there were between 800 and 1000 mergers each year, of which about 120 met one or other of the statutory tests.

SUMMARY

Monopoly

Problems   a Monopoly can and may lead to higher prices, lower output and inflexibilities in the industrial structure.

        b Big firms can offer greater efficiency and economies of scale, and collusion can sometimes contribute to greater efficiency.

Policy   a Official agencies can do much to promote rationalisation, integration, and better pricing, marketing and wage-fixing procedures.

        b There must be safeguards against the abuse of monopoly power.

Effects   The multiplicity of aims led to the creation of several official bodies with some overlapping of functions and a possibility of conflict. Recent legislation has created an institution to coordinate the work in this field.

The Institutions

Monopolies and Mergers Commission   Founded 1948. Functions: Investigates, reports and makes recommendations on large firm monopolies, mergers, monopolies in service industries, and on restrictive practices not subject to registration.

Restrictive Practices Court;   Founded 1956. Functions: To decide whether registered restrictive practices are likely to operate against the public interest, and to make judgements on any breaches of the Court's rulings.

The Office of the Director-General of Fair Trading.   Set up in 1973. Functions: To maintain a continuous scrutiny of consumer affairs, receive complaints, initiate investigations, and make references to the Consumer Protection Advisory Committee. To recommend appropriate action to the Secretary of State. To carry out preliminary studies and make references to the Monopolies and Mergers Commission. To maintain the register of restrictive agreements and make references to the Restrictive Practices Court.

The Legislation

1948   *The Monopolies and Restrictive Practices Act*
Set up Monopolies Commission with powers to investigate, report, and recommend.

1953   *The Monopolies and Restrictive Practices Act*
Strengthened Monopolies Commission — membership increased ten to twenty-five members — permitted to work in groups on several cases simultaneously.

1956   *The Restrictive Trade Practices Act*
  a Required registration and judicial investigation of restrictive practices;
  b collective RPM made illegal, but individual RPM made legally enforceable;
  c reduced size (twenty-five to ten members) and role of Monopolies Commission.

1964   *The Resale Prices Act*
  All forms of RPM made illegal — agreements placed on register may continue until brought before the Court.

1965   *The Monopolies and Mergers Act*
  Monopolies Commission enlarged to twenty-five members and right to work in groups restored; commission's powers extended to, (a) investigate monopolies in service industries and (b) investigate mergers and proposed mergers.

1968   *The Restrictive Practices Act*
  Department of Trade and Industry given power to (a) exempt certain restrictive agreements from registration and (b) call for the registration of information agreements; additional 'gateway' introduced.

1973   *The Fair Trading Act*
  Established the office of the Director-General of Fair Trading with overall responsibility for the implementation of the government's policy on competition, monopolies and mergers; monopoly re-defined as situation where one-quarter of total market is under unified control; nationalised industries and local monopolies subject to investigation; provisions for speeding up monopoly enquiries; definition of public interest extended to include need for more competition.

Reports of the Monopolies Commission

	Title	*House of Commons Paper No.*
1	Supply and export of matches and the supply of match-making machinery	161 (1952–53)
2	Supply of electric lamps	287 (1950–51)
3	Supply of insulated electric wires and cables	209 (1951–52)
4	Supply of cast iron rainwater goods	136 (1950–51)
5	Supply of dental goods	18 (1950–51)
6	Supply and export of certain semi-manufactures of copper and copper-based alloys	56 (1955–56)
7	Supply of insulin	296 (1951–52)
8	Process of calico printing	140 (1953–54)
9	Supply of imported timber	281 (1952–53)
10	Supply and export of electrical and allied machinery and plant	42 (1956–57)
11	Supply and export of pneumatic tyres	133 (1955–56)

64	Connection charges for electricity and gas	Cmnd 5036 (July 1972)
65	Supply of fire insurance	396 (2.8.72)
66	Supply of asbestos and certain asbestos products	3 (23.1.73)
67	A Report on the Supply of Ready Cooked Breakfast Cereal Foods	2 (20.2.73)
68	A Report on the Supply of Chlordiazepoxide and Diazepam	197 (11.4.73)
69	A Report on the Supply and Export of Machinery for the Manufacture of Footwear	215 (2.5.73)
70	A Report on the General Effect on the Public Interest of the Practice of Parallel Pricing	Cmnd. 5330 (July 73)
71	A Report on the Proposed Merger British Match Corporation Ltd. and Wilkinson Sword Ltd.	Cmnd 5442 (Oct 73)
72	A Report on the proposed transfer of eighteen newspapers owned by Kentish Times Ltd., Gravesend and Dartford Reporter Ltd. and F. J. Parsons Ltd. to Westminster Press Ltd.	460 (25.10.73)
73	A Report on the Supply and Exports of Wire Rope and Fibre and Cordage	2 (20.11.73)
74	A report on the Supply of Plasterboard	94 (21.1.74)
75	A Report on the Supply of certain Cross-Channel Car Ferry services	14 (10.4.74)
76	A Report on the Supply of Primary Batteries	880 (7.11.74)

The Restrictive Practices Court — Contested Cases

Case	Date	Decision
Chemists	Nov. 1958	Contrary
Yarn Spinners	Jan. 1959	Contrary
Blankets	Mar. 1959	Contrary (with small exception)
Scottish Bakers	July 1959	Contrary
Water Tube Boilers	July 1959	Not Contrary
Wholesale and Multiple Bakers	Dec. 1959	Contrary
Carpets	Dec. 1959	Contrary
Phenol	Apr. 1960	Contrary
Black Bolts and Nuts (1) (ordinary user agreement)	July 1960	Not Contrary
Doncaster and Retford Co-op.	Oct. 1960	Contrary
Wholesale Confectioners	Dec. 1960	Contrary
Motor Vehicle Distributors	Dec. 1960	Contrary
Transformers (1)	Mar. 1961	Contrary
Cement	Mar. 1961	Not Contrary
Bottles	Mar. 1961	Contrary
Linoleum	June 1961	Contrary
Newspapers	July 1961	Contrary
Permanent Magnets	June 1962	Not Contrary

Case	Date	Decision
Metal Windows	July 1962	Not Contrary
Net Books (RPM Agreement)	Oct. 1962	Not Contrary
Jute	Mar. 1963	Contrary
Tyre Trade	Mar. 1963	Contrary
Birmingham Builders	Apr. 1963	Contrary
Waste Paper	Apr. 1963	Contrary
Sulphuric Acid Ass. (1)	July 1963	Not Contrary
Glazed Tiles	Jan. 1964	Not Contrary
Steel Scrap	Jan. 1964	Not Contrary
Heavy Steel	June 1964	Contrary
Mining and Locked Coil Ropes	Dec. 1964	Contrary
Finance Houses	Oct. 1965	Contrary
Black Bolts and Nuts (2) (large user agreement)	Dec. 1965	Not Contrary
Fish	Nov. 1966	Not Contrary
Sulphuric Acid Ass. (2)	Nov. 1966	Not Contrary
Chocolate and Sugar Confectionery (RPM Agreement)	July 1967	Contrary
Footwear (RPM Agreement)	June 1968	Contrary
National Federation of Newsagents and Booksellers	May 1969	Contrary
Mallaig and Northwest Fishermen (quota agreement)	March 1970	Contrary
Medicaments (RPM Agreement)	June 1970	Not Contrary
Electrical Installation at Exeter Hospital (tendering agreement)	July 1970	Contrary
Transformers (2) (application to establish new agreement)	October 1970	Granted
Japanese Canned Food	Nov. 1971	Contrary
Scottish Daily Newspapers	July 1972	Not Contrary
Flushing Cisterns	May 1973	Contrary

Note: The great majority of the successful cases used gateway 'b', i.e. the public derived specific and substantial benefits.

APPENDIX 1

RESTRICTIVE PRACTICES COURT

Standard Metal Windows Group's Agreement
Judgement given 17th July 1962

The case concerned an agreement between firms manufacturing standard metal windows. The agreement bound the member firms to:

    a operate an agreed delivered price system with agreed rebates for quantity orders;

    b operate a restriction limiting the amounts of any discount, rebate, cash bonus or other consideration to those stated in the agreement;

    c observe an agreed allowance of 10% on inter-trading between member firms;

    d enforce resale price maintenance.

The group chose to defend their agreement on the grounds that its abrogation would deny specific and substantial benefits to the public. They argued that, as a result of the agreement:

    a prices of standard metal windows have been, are, and will be lower than they would otherwise have been;

    b the quality of the windows the the services provided by the manufacturers is and will be better than would be the case without such an agreement;

    c the purchasers have had and will have a wider choice of supplies.

On the evidence presented the Court decided that points b and c were not proven and it decided to judge the case on the evidence in support of case a.

The major point in the defence of the agreement lay in the argument that the agreement to limit price competition has led to most effective technical collaboration between the member firms under which there was a full exchange of cost data, time studies, information on developments in technique, machinery, layout of plant, and economy in the use of men and materials. The Court accepted the evidence here as most convincing and said that the exchange of information on costs was more detailed and comprehensive than in any other industry known to the expert witnesses used by the Court. This collaboration it was held had been effective in keeping down costs and in improving design and quality. Again, this was accepted by the Court, although the Registrar pointed out that the stimulus from competition between members might also have led to similar improvements in efficiency. The Court, however, was influenced by the fact that the group was already subject to keen price competition from firms outside the group — from manufacturers of wooden windows, and from Crittalls, a large firm manufacturing metal windows which was not party to the agreement. Crittalls, in fact, held 43% of the market in metal windows while members of the group accounted for 42%.

Accepting the evidence that members' costs had been lower in the past than they would have been had there been no restrictive agreement, the Court then asked whether this was also true of prices. Again, the Court accepted the group's argument that this was so. Since the market was extremely competitive prices were closely related to costs and because the group had kept costs lower than they would otherwise have been, the members of the group had been more effective competitors in the markets for windows to the benefit of the purchasers.

The next question to be considered was whether the exchange of cost data and technical information would continue if the agreement were to be condemned. The firms said that it would not, and the Court was satisfied that although a price war would be unlikely, abandonment of the agreement would lead to a substantial lessening of technical co-operation with a resulting reduction in future savings of costs among members.

The Court then considered the likely future impact on prices if the agreement ceased to operate. Some witnesses thought there would be an increase in competition which would lower prices, but the Court took the opposite view. It thought that competition would be more effective if the group were allowed to continue. If the group were broken up, members would be in a weaker position so far as sustained competition was concerned and the manufacturing costs of each member would be higher.

The judgement of the Court was that a specific and substantial benefit to purchasers or users of windows derived from the operation of the agreement.

With regard to the second hurdle the Court was satisfied that any detriments to non-parties and the public were outweighed by the benefits.

Decision: *Not Contrary*

APPENDIX 2

THE MONOPOLIES COMMISSION

A Summary of Findings and Conclusions on the Supply and Processing of Colour Film

(Presented April 1966)

1 Market shares

The total sales of colour film in the United Kingdom in 1964 were worth about £15m, about £10m of this being the income of manufacturers, importers and processors. Of this £10m, slightly more than half was attributable to the sale of film and the rest to the service of processing. Kodak was responsible for about three-quarters of the sales of film and for some two-thirds of the processing, that is, about 70% of the total trade covered by the reference. In 1962, the next largest share was held by Ilford with about 10% of the market, but by 1964 this had fallen to about 4½% and Agfa were then in second place with about 11% of the market. Apart from the Eastern Bloc and Japan, the world market for colour film is largely supplied by five groups, three of them American controlled. All these groups sell their products on the world market. Only two firms manufacture colour film in the United Kingdom — Kodak and Ilford, but the other makes are available in this country (at the time of the report there was an import tariff of about 20% on colour film).

2 Bases of monopoly power

This is an industry where the successful firm must be prepared to invest very large sums in costly research and experimentation towards long term improvement of its product, in plant for large scale production (to reduce costs to levels which ensure a mass market), and in sales promotion to develop that market. It was inevitable, therefore, that the colour film market in Britain should fall into the hands of a very small number of suppliers. When colour film was first introduced in the 1930s Kodak had already been making photographic material here for more than forty years. It had the technical and financial backing of Eastman Kodak which dominates the American and many other markets, and its established reputation was a valuable asset in promoting the new product. Its success was also due to its high standards of technical and commercial enterprise and efficiency. The patenting of inventions may also have played some part in establishing and maintaining Kodak's dominance in this field. Other factors which might help to explain this situation are, the effects of the war on competitors some of which, unlike Kodak's parent company, were unable to maintain their activities in amateur colour photography, and the existence of the UK tariff which provided some degree of protection.

3 Effects of the monopoly position
a Profits and Prices
The colour film business accounted for about one-sixth, by value, of Kodak's business, but it was responsible for about one-third of total net profits. The Commission thought that the profits on colour film were unduly high. The table below shows the commission's calculations of profits on capital employed by Kodak.

	1962	1963	1964
Colour Film Business	44.1%	51.7%	55.6%
Other Business	14.6%	16.2%	17.6%

Kodak argued:
  i that it was difficult, if not impossible, to derive accurate figures for the profitability of any one product;
  ii that it had very little freedom in setting prices since it was in competition with powerful international rivals;
  iii it was misleading to isolate the profitability of any one product line since, in any multi-product firm, the profitability of different lines will vary, and only overall profits can be taken as a valid basis for judgement;
  iv it was entitled to fairly high profits on a product which was the result of expensive research and development.

The Commission, however, thought that Kodak's position made it a price leader with considerable discretion to set prices for itself and others. It suggested that Kodak's market dominance was being used to earn disproportionately high profits and recommended that the firm should substantially reduce its selling prices for colour film. The fact that this might well tend to enhance Kodak's monopoly position did not disturb the Commission which pointed out that monopoly could be advantageous to the public if it resulted in economies of scale which were passed on to the customer.

b Practices
The Commission criticised Kodak's policy of confining the retail distribution of its products to certain appointed outlets as being a limitation on competition and a means of maintaining unduly high retail margins (about 30% at the time of the report). The practice of selling Kodachrome at prices which included the cost of

processing was regarded as a restriction of competition and consumer choice although the Commission recognised the technical difficulties — processing required expensive equipment, expertise and large scale operation. Nevertheless the Commission thought that both these practices could be considered to operate against the public interest.

c Remedies

Kodak's monopoly position itself does not operate against the public interest and certain objectionable practices could be eliminated without damaging the company's dominant position. The Commission recommended:

  i the abolition of the import duty on colour film;
 ii a significant reduction in Kodak's selling prices for colour film and in the charges for processing;
iii a reduction in the distributors' margins on colour film;
 iv that Kodak should permit its colour film to be stocked and sold by any retailer who wished to deal in it (subject to normal commercial considerations of credit-worthiness);
  v that retailers should be free to supply colour film on a process-paid basis or not as the customer requires, and there should be no recommended retail price for processing;
 vi that the manufacturers should be prepared to supply technical help to independent processors where it was requested.

d Results

After discussions with the Board of Trade, Kodak agreed to make a reduction of 12½%, on average, in the prices of their colour films to the retailer. They also agreed to abandon any restriction on the supply of colour film to retail outlets. Kodak and other suppliers agreed to introduce arrangements which would enable retailers to sell reversible colour film either inclusive of a charge for processing or not, at the consumer's choice. These suppliers also indicated their willingness to consider requests for technical help from independent processors.

The Board of Trade did not agree to reduce or abolish the tariff on colour film.

One result of the price reductions has been that Ilford Ltd. has abandoned the retail market in colour films.

EXERCISES

The following activities may be suitable for group projects or individual assignments. They should be treated as suggestions which may be modified to suit the resources of time and materials available.

1 Using some of the recommended sources of reference (e.g. the Annual Report of the Dept. of Trade on Monopolies and Mergers, and the Reports of the Monopolies Commission) prepare either a large display chart or a suitably indexed booklet to record a summary of the reports on monopoly situations, extracting in each case

a the market shares of the firms investigated,

b the level of profits on capital employed with some suitable comparison with those for say, manufacturing industry as a whole,

c the nature of the barriers to entry,

d the recommendations,

e subsequent action.

2 Using the material obtained in Exercise 1, extract the relevant data in order to reveal

a the variety and frequency of the barriers to entry,

b the variety and frequency of the Commission's suggestions for controlling monopoly situations.

e.g. *Measures to control monopoly – Commission's suggestions*

Method	Report
i Abolition or reduction of import tariff	i Supply of colour film
	ii Supply of man-made cellulosic fibres
	iii etc.

3 Using appropriate sources of reference (e.g. Reports of the Registrar of Restrictive Agreements, and articles in *The Economist* and *The Times*), prepare a summary chart of hearings before the Restrictive Practices Court identifying:

a the nature of the restrictive practice;

b the defence arguments and the gateway chosen by the defence;

c the Registrar's arguments;

d the decision.

It might be interesting to supplement this work by preparing some kind of simple frequency chart (e.g. in the form of a histogram) to illustrate diagrammatically the frequency of certain types of restrictive practice and the different gateways used by the firms and trade associations

4 Using the Dept. of Trade's Annual Reports on Monopolies and

Mergers and current press reports keep a diary or wall chart showing:

a proposed mergers and take over bids;

b action by the Dept. of Trade (i.e. whether referred to the Commission or not);

c the findings of the Commission;

d subsequent action.

Again, this might be supported by statistical analysis to show say,

e number of mergers effected each year;

f percentage of these referred to the Commission;

g percentage of those referred to the Commission which are not approved;

h some breakdown of the mergers into broad industrial groupings to show the incidence of mergers in the different sectors of the economy.

5 Using some suitable book in the local reference library (e.g. *Who Owns Whom*) find some very large companies which have many subsidiaries. Prepare 'family trees' indicating the industries to which each of the subsidiaries belongs. Is the organisation a conglomerate of a closely integrated group within an industry? Are there examples of both horizontal and vertical integration in the structure?

6 On visits to local firms try to discover whether the firm is a 'price taker' or 'price maker'. Does it manufacture for say, 'the £2.50 market', or does it have considerable freedom in setting its prices? Prepare a report on the relevant market features and compare it with the necessary conditions for:

a perfect competition;

b monopoly;

c oligopoly;

d monopolistic competition.

7 Using the excellent material supplied by the European Economic Community (23 Chesham Street, London SW1) prepare a summary of the major features of the Community's policies on monopolies and mergers and contrast it with the current British position.

8 A Mock Hearing before the Monopolies Commission.

Choose two local firms or two firms on which you can obtain the necessary information (e.g. from their annual reports and statements of accounts) and prepare a case for a merger between them. One group of students should present the case for the merger, and another group should act as the Commission by asking searching and relevant questions followed by a statement giving the recommendations. The rest of the group may act as 'the Dept. of Trade' by giving the final decision.

9 Obtain the annual reports of the IRC and examine its activities
   in the promotion of mergers. Outline:
   a the IRC's motives;
   b the nature of its assistance;
   c the likely effects of the merger;
   d any likely clash of interests with the Monopolies Commis-
      sion.

10 Many large companies publish an abbreviated statement of their
   annual accounts (and Chairman's statement) in the national
   press. These statements often include a list of subsidiary
   companies and their activities. Some companies will provide
   copies of their annual statements free of charge. Using these
   sources try to develop a 'map' of some typical conglomerate
   and then try to discover some economic logic in its structure,
   e.g. firms may produce very different commodities but have
   common channels of distribution (cigarettes and potato crisps!)

GINN AND COMPANY LTD
Elsinore House, Buckingham Street, Aylesbury, Bucks HP20 2NQ

SATELLITE TEXTS

The Manchester Economics Project consists of a series of books and visual aids, forming an integrated scheme for the study of economics at G.C.E. 'A' Level and its equivalents. This booklet is a satellite text designed to be used with the central textbook of theory, *Understanding Economics*, but it can be used in conjunction with any sound textbook of economics. Other titles are listed inside the back cover.

© G. Stanlake 1970
Revised edition 1976   027612
Product No. 568546725   ISBN 0 602 22339 3
Printed by Express Litho Service (Oxford)